Girlfriends walk through life together, whether they live close or far apart. They know that the other one is there... to share the highs and the lows and everything else. They are connected at the heart.

— Donna Fargo

Blue Mountain Arts®

New and Best-Selling Titles

By Susan Polis Schutz:
To My Daughter with Love on the Important Things in Life
To My Son with Love

By Douglas Pagels:
For You, My Soul Mate
Required Reading for All Teenagers
The Next Chapter of Your Life
You Are One Amazing Lady

By Marci:
Angels Are Everywhere!
Friends Are Forever
10 Simple Things to Remember
To My Daughter
To My Granddaughter
To My Son
You Are My "Once in a Lifetime"

By Wally Amos, with Stu Glauberman:
The Path to Success Is Paved with Positive Thinking

By Minx Boren:
Healing Is a Journey

By Carol Wiseman:
Emerging from the Heartache of Loss

Anthologies:
A Daughter Is Life's Greatest Gift
A Daybook of Positive Thinking
A Son Is Life's Greatest Gift
Dream Big, Stay Positive, and Believe in Yourself
Girlfriends Are the Best Friends of All
God Is Always Watching Over You
God Loves You Just the Way You Are
Hang In There
The Love Between a Mother and Daughter Is Forever
Nothing Fills the Heart with Joy like a Grandson
There Is Nothing Sweeter in Life Than a Granddaughter
There Is So Much to Love About You... Daughter
Think Positive Thoughts Every Day
When I Say I Love You
Words Every Woman Should Remember

Girlfriends

Are the

Best Friends of All

A Blue Mountain Arts®
Collection

Edited by Patricia Wayant

Blue Mountain Press™

Boulder, Colorado

Library of Congress Control Number: 2011903233
ISBN: 978-1-59842-872-8 (previously ISBN: 978-1-59842-603-8)

� and Blue Mountain Press are registered in U.S. Patent and Trademark Office. Certain trademarks are used under license.

Acknowledgments appear on page 124.

Printed in China.
First printing of this edition: 2015

✪ This book is printed on recycled paper.

This book is printed on paper that has been specially produced to be acid free (neutral pH) and contains no groundwood or unbleached pulp. It conforms with the requirements of the American National Standards Institute, Inc., so as to ensure that this book will last and be enjoyed by future generations.

Blue Mountain Arts, Inc.
P.O. Box 4549, Boulder, Colorado 80306

Contents

A Girlfriend Is
the Best Friend of All

A girlfriend is the one person on this earth
you feel whole with,
the one you share who you really are with.
She knows where you're coming from,
all you've been through,
and everything you're dreaming about.
She is the one you tell anything to,
ask anything of,
and do anything for.

She's the one you tell all your truths to,
the one you give your whole heart to.
She is absolute acceptance,
abiding affection, and unconditional caring.
Just spending a moment with her
chases your cares away
and puts a smile on your face.
She always knows what you need
and when you need it
in a way no one else does...

A girlfriend understands what you hope for,
what you believe in,
and what you are committed to.
She is your sunshine and shadow friend —
constant, enduring, and absolute.
She is the one who believes in you,
who accepts you and respects you,
the one you can call on anytime,
the one who never lets you down.

She fills a unique space in your life.
She's a piece of your very heart and soul,
and because of her you know
without a doubt
that love can get you through anything.

A girlfriend is the best friend of all.

— Vickie M. Worsham

Our Girlfriends Keep Us Sane

Girlfriends are all ears when we need them to listen. They lend us a hand if we need their help. They're generous, and they'll give us the shirts off their backs if they know we want them. They're fun to hang out with, talk silly about nothing with, shop with, and cheat on our diets with.

They understand our feelings and show us acceptance and perspective. They acknowledge our efforts when we're trying hard. They help relieve the pressure of everyday life just by always being there.

What would we do without our girlfriends to complain to and act so crazy with? They're sensitive to our moods, and they stand by us when we need them to. They lend us their shoulders to cry on. They laugh with us when life's not all that funny and we get caught in some mess. They lift us and encourage us and support us. They're our refuge in this unfriendly world, our buddies to walk with through the storms.

— Donna Fargo

What a Difference a Girlfriend Makes!

Girlfriends are always so willing
to go that extra mile and do
whatever it takes
to make someone else's life
a little bit brighter.
Their special blend of caring
goes a long way toward proving
there are still kindhearted people
in this world —
people who seem to receive
their greatest joy
by sharing the best of themselves
with others.

— Cindy Chuksudoon

If you're ever doubting yourself, your girlfriend will remind you that you are strong, smart, and beautiful... and that you can do anything.

— Anna Marie Edwards

Girlfriends bring out the brilliance and beauty in each other's spirit and shine together forever like two bright stars.

— Anna Jakobs

I Don't Know What I'd Do Without Her

If it weren't for her, I wouldn't have half as much laughter or nearly as much joy. I wouldn't have as much peace or understanding. And I definitely wouldn't have as much fun!

I love that she's there. And whether it's in person or on the phone... I love the connection that is always there between us.

What we share is really something special. I feel more at home with her than I do with just about anyone, and feelings like those are some of the most precious of all.

Our friendship will always mean so much to me.

It is simply and sweetly... the best there is.

— Ann Turrell

I'm So Thankful for My Girlfriends

Friendship begins with meeting someone along the path of life — someone you get to know, and gradually get to know even better. You discover what a joy it is to spend your moments with this person.

It's nice the way the good feelings of friendship remain. The happiness lasts, and the memories you make start to turn into some of your favorite treasures. Friendship is two paths converging on the way to the same beautiful view. Friendship is walking the way together.

Friendship is opening up to one another. It's sharing thoughts and feelings in a way that never felt very comfortable before. It is a complete trust, sweetened with a lot more understanding and communication than many people will ever know.

Friendship is two hearts that share and that are able to say things no outsiders ever could. Friendship is an inner door that only a friend has the key to. Friendship is a gift, continually giving happiness. It is strong and supportive, and few things in all the world will ever compare with the joy that comes from its wonderful bond.

— Mia Evans

What's So Special About Girlfriends?

Girlfriends bring casseroles and scrub your bathroom
    when you are sick.
Girlfriends keep your children and keep your secrets.
Girlfriends give advice when you ask for it.
    Sometimes you take it, sometimes you don't.

Girlfriends don't always tell you that you're right,
   but they're usually honest.
Girlfriends still love you, even when they don't agree
   with your choices.
Girlfriends might send you a birthday card, but they
   might not. It does not matter in the least.
Girlfriends laugh with you, and you don't need canned
   jokes to start the laughter.
Girlfriends pull you out of jams.
Girlfriends don't keep a calendar that lets them know
   who hosted the other last.
Girlfriends are there for you, in an instant and truly,
   when the hard times come.
                                    — Author Unknown

Girlfriends Are Great Because...

- A girlfriend always has time for you no matter what.

- She's the first person you want to call when something funny, scary, or crazy happens.

- You can tell your girlfriend things you'd never tell anyone else.

- A girlfriend fills your heart with happiness.

- A girlfriend knows your dreams, your strengths, and your hopes.

- She knows your quirks, your bad habits, and your insecurities.

- She knows what makes you tick, what makes you crazy, and what makes you smile.

- She knows when to talk, when to listen, and when to make you laugh.

- A girlfriend knows you better than anyone else does.

A Girlfriend Is
One of Life's
Most Beautiful Gifts

She is a person you can trust,
who won't turn away from you.
She will be there
when you really need someone
and will come to you when she needs help.
She will listen to you
even when she doesn't understand
or agree with your feelings.

She will never try to change you
but appreciates you for who you are.
She doesn't expect too much
or give too little;
she is someone you can share
dreams, hopes, and feelings with.
She is a person you can think of
and suddenly smile;
she doesn't have to be told
that she is special,
because she knows you feel that way.
She will accept your attitudes,
ideas, and emotions,
even when her own are different;
she will hold your hand
when you're scared.
She will be honest with you
even when it might hurt
and will forgive you
for the mistakes you make...

A girlfriend can never disappoint you
and will support you
and share in your glory.
She shares responsibility
when you have doubts.
She always remembers
the little things you've done,
the times you've shared,
and the talks you've had.
She will bend over backward
to help you pick up the pieces
when your world falls apart.
A girlfriend is one of life's
most beautiful gifts.

— Luann Auciello

Friends are cherished people
we carry in our hearts
wherever we go in life.
They are the unforgettable people
we dream and plan
great futures with,
who accept us as we are,
and encourage us to become
all that we want to be.

— Donna Levine-Small

My Girlfriends Mean the World to Me

We discuss so openly
the many personal aspects of our lives.
We talk about our needs,
our dreams,
our similarities and differences.
We give one another
the freedom to ask anything
and talk about everything.
We put all our concerns in the open,
so that we have the freedom
to grow and be ourselves.

We can tell one another anything,
no matter how personal
or how much it might hurt.
We never hold one another down;
we respect each other,
and we laugh together.

These are just a few of the reasons
why my girlfriends mean
the world to me.

— Sherrie L. Householder

A Girlfriend's Bill of Rights

1. A girlfriend has the right to borrow money, clothes, junk food, or any combination thereof at any time, provided that such borrowing has been approved in advance.

2. In any given crisis situation (e.g., lost keys, lost purse, lost boyfriend), a girlfriend has the right to call at any time, including 2:00 a.m., no matter how trivial the crisis may seem the next day.

3. A girlfriend has the right to convey top-secret information without risk of information being disclosed to other friends, boyfriends, or anyone else of importance.

4. In the event that one girlfriend is trying on jeans at a store, the observing friend has the right to indicate when such jeans are not flattering. In the event that jeans have already been purchased and taken home from store, the observing friend has the right, and duty, to insist that said jeans look fabulous no matter what.

5. When in the presence of her friend, a girlfriend has the right, as needed, to cry so hard that she needs an entire box of tissues or laugh so hard that her drink squirts out her nose.

6. A girlfriend has the right, at any time, to hug her friend for any reason... or for no reason at all.

— Melissa Simpson

Rare People

There are many people
that we meet in our lives
but only a very few
will make a lasting impression
on our minds and hearts

These people will always
listen and talk to you
They will care about your happiness
   and well-being
They will like you for who you are
and they will support you at all times
It is these rare people that we will
think of often
and who will always remain
important to us
as true friends

— Susan Polis Schutz

No Explanation Needed!

Your girlfriend is someone who listens without judging you. Right or wrong, good or bad, she gently helps you define your thoughts to regain perspective.

When you're feeling bad about yourself, she reminds you of all those positive qualities you may have forgotten. She loves you for who you are, not for what you do.

She gives you the priceless gift of time: time to share, to try out new ideas, and to rethink old ones.

Together, you learn the fine art of giving. You expand, become more selfless, feel more deeply, and help more effectively. Seeing the happiness you bring to another person gives you a greater sense of well-being and increases your capacity to love.

Wherever you go in life, whatever stage or place you reach, this friend who has entered your soul is always with you — gently guiding, faithfully following, and ever walking beside you.

— Sandra Sturtz Hauss

A Feeling in the Heart

There's a special bond
between girlfriends
that cannot be understood
by others —
a unique love that
goes far beyond
a simple feeling of the heart.

It gives me great peace to know
I can always count on my girlfriend
to say or do just what I most need
at any given moment;
she's always ready to give
a hug, a kind word,
or the gentle urging I sometimes need
to keep moving forward.
I don't know what I'd ever do
without our precious friendship.

— Julie Gridley Crosby

The Depth of Friendship

"Friend."
Some people take this word for granted.
They use it to describe almost anyone
who touches their lives.
But that's not fair,
for not everyone fits this word.
It is easy to be a pal, a buddy,
a companion, or an acquaintance,
but to be a friend means so very much more.

To be a friend
means being trusted and trusting,
honest and dedicated,
supportive and available.
It means going strong with
your own life's work and plans,
yet reaching out to another when you're needed
(and maybe even when you're not).

To be a friend is to be fun and fair,
serious and silly.
It's to make the mundane exciting,
the unexpected acceptable,
to be the silent stronghold without being asked,
to feel happy for someone else's happiness, and
to share the burden of sorrow in thought and action.

The qualifications of being a friend
are too high for the ordinary to reach.
It takes a while to earn the title
and a lifetime to truly know its meaning.
Never take the job lightly or give it away too quickly;
it must be cultivated, nurtured, and cared for.
For when you truly find a "friend,"
you are lucky enough to have one for life.

— Laura V. Nicholson

To a Special Friend

You have known me
in good and
bad times
You have seen me
when I was happy
and when I was sad
You have listened to me
when what I said was intelligent
and when I talked nonsense
You have been with me
when we had fun
and when we were miserable
You have watched me
laugh
and cry

You have understood me
when I knew what I was doing
and when I made mistakes
Thank you for
believing in me
for supporting me
and for always being ready
to share thoughts together
You are a perfect friend

— Susan Polis Schutz

Girlfriends Have Fun Together

◎ Girlfriends have many adventures together — whether it's salsa lessons, pottery classes, or just a "girls' night out."

◎ They know how to make boring activities fun... and fun activities a blast.

◎ They are the first to hit the dance floor.

◎ They make the world's best road-trip buddies, hands down!

- Girlfriends sing together at the top of their lungs when a good song comes on the radio.

- They are must-have companions when you're shopping for bathing suits or jeans.

- They are the perfect people to take silly pictures with in a photo booth.

- Your girlfriends are always your "girl" friends, no matter how old you both may be.

Never a Dull Moment

Our friendship has always been
the kind that lets us talk
and tell each other anything.
We've always gathered our thoughts
    and feelings
and laid them at each other's doorstep.
As friends, we've shared a million
    memories —
some sad and many happy ones.
We've opened those special places
    in the heart
where only best friends are welcome.

We've been through thick and thin together.
We've done our best to bring hope
    to each other
when it looked like all hope was gone.
We've cheered each other on until
    a tiny smile was born.
We've always been open and honest
    with each other;
we've had the kind of friendship
    that most people never find.

As long as we're friends,
life's never going to be lonely, boring,
or without someone special.
Our friendship means so much to me.

— Barbara J. Hall

Girlfriends Weave Our World

Any woman who sews
or knits or weaves,
who blends colors in a tapestry
or creates a patchwork quilt,
knows by the feel
that a single thread is weak,
but the weaving,
the blending,
the intertwining
with many others
make it strong.

Any woman alone —
without friends
to sustain her,
to nurture and support her,
to hold her with loving arms —
like a single thread, is weak.
But the weaving,
the loving,
the nurturing of others,
the networks of friendship
make her strong.

— Author Unknown

Women Change the World Every Day

There are women who make things better...
simply by showing up. There are women who
make things happen. There are women who
make their way. There are women who make a
difference. And women who make us smile. There
are women who do not make excuses. Women who
cannot be replaced. There are women of wit and
wisdom who — through strength and courage —
make it through. There are women who change
the world every day.

— Ashley Rice

What do we live for, if it is not to make life less difficult for each other?

— George Eliot
(Mary Anne Evans)

Let Me Tell You About My Best Friend

She's the one person
   who shares my deepest thoughts
and loves me in spite of them.
She counsels me when my heart is broken,
and she stands by me when I'm mistreated.
She rallies behind me in my good decisions
and is there to help me through
   the consequences of the bad ones.
Who else can I call at any hour
   of the day or night?
Who else accepts and understands all of me?
Not many people are as blessed as I am
with someone like her in their lives.

I don't know why the heavens decided
    to give me
the wonderful gift of her as my friend,
but I'm grateful.
No matter what comes along, good or bad,
it brings me great comfort and security
to know that I can always count on her.
I hope she knows in her heart that
I am that same sort of friend to her.
Our secrets are safe and our hearts
    are protected
because of the love between us...
two special friends.

— Pamela Malone-Melton

Top Ten Things
Only Women Understand

10. Why it's good to have five pairs of black shoes.

9. The difference between cream, ivory, and off-white.

8. Crying can be fun.

7. Fat clothes.

6. A salad, diet drink, and a hot fudge sundae make a balanced lunch.

5. Why discovering a designer dress on the clearance rack can be considered a peak life experience.

4. A good man might be hard to find, but a good hairdresser is next to impossible.

3. The inaccuracy of every bathroom scale ever made.

2. Why a phone call between two women never lasts under ten minutes.

And the number one thing only women understand:

1. Other women!

— Author Unknown

Girlfriends Speak a Language Only Women Understand

Women don't need a lot of schooling to understand each other. We can sense each other's disappointment about our hurts, failings, and regrets, and we know when we're playing games and just putting on a happy face.

We can cut to the chase with our blatant honesty, because we're the kind of friends who are trusted, tried, and true. We're sensitive to each other's feelings about our imperfections, and because we know each other so well, we don't have to say a word sometimes. We just know instinctively when to reach out or be quiet and say nothing.

We put up with one another when we're not always the easiest to be with. We accept and respect and forgive. We have empathy when one of us is having a hard time with something. We appreciate each other's thoughtfulness, but most of all, we are loyal and understanding.

In the language of girlfriends, we're awesome!

— Donna Fargo

Thank You for Being My Friend

When things are confused
I discuss them with you
until they make sense

When something good happens
you are the first person I tell
so I can share my happiness

When I don't know what to do in a situation
I ask your opinion
and weigh it heavily with mine

When I am lonely
I call you
because I never feel alone with you

When I have a problem
I ask for your help
because your wisdom helps me to solve it

When I want to have fun
I want to be with you
because we have such a great time together

When I want to talk to someone
I always talk to you
because you understand me

When I want the truth about something
I call you
because you are so honest

It is so essential
to have you in my life
Thank you for being my friend

— Susan Polis Schutz

Girlfriends Are...

- ◉ Generous.

- ◉ Sweet.

- ◉ Beautiful.

- ◉ Hilarious.

- ◉ Compassionate.

- ◉ Sincere.

- ◉ Smart.

- ◉ Patient.

- ◉ Accepting.

- ◉ Reliable.

There is no need for
an outpouring of words
to explain oneself
to a friend
Friends understand each
other's thoughts even
before they are spoken
— Susan Polis Schutz

Knowing that you are always
here to understand and accept
me helps me get along in the
confused world. If every person
could have someone just like
you, the world would become
a peaceful garden.
— Susan Polis Schutz

Girlfriends Just Know...

They know just the right
   thing to say or do;
they can make you feel better
   just by being near;
they listen with an open heart
   and understand.
They laugh with you when you're happy;
they share your tears when you're sad;
they are there beside you
   whenever you feel alone;
they extend their hand when
   you need support;
they are proud of all that
   you accomplish;
they love you just because you're you.

— Geri Danks

You know how I feel
You listen to how I think
You understand...
You're my friend

— Susan Polis Schutz

One Amazing Lady

My girlfriend is one amazing lady. She's so good to the people in her life. So considerate and caring. When she gives, it's easy to see that it comes straight from the heart... and it gives everyone around her the gift of a nicer world to live in.

I love how strong she is inside. I always see that quality shine in her, and it reassures me to know — even though she faces hardships and uncertainties just like many people do — there's a way through and a brighter day ahead. She's my reminder to be a little more brave, to not be so afraid, and to remember that things will turn out okay in the long run.

I love the way she doesn't let the crazy, difficult days get her down. I admire her ability to put things in perspective. To laugh when she can. To cry when she must. But always to try to make things better.

To her friends, she is everything a friend should be. To her family, she is dearly loved and truly the best.

She is such a deserving person. And I treasure just being in this world with her.

— Lorrie Westfall

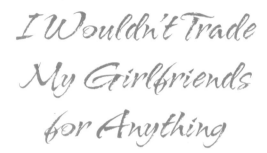

I Wouldn't Trade My Girlfriends for Anything

- When a girlfriend asks, "How are you?" she's not just being polite — she really wants to know.

- Girlfriends always want to hear all the details.

- They can talk for hours and never run out of things to say.

- Girlfriends feel perfectly comfortable sitting together in silence, too.

- They help you make important decisions.

- They offer great advice, valuable insights, and unique points of view.

- They believe in each other.

- They stand up for each other.

- You can call your girlfriends anytime, day or night.

All I Need to Know in Life I Learned from My Girlfriends

- Good times are even better when they're shared.

- A long talk can cure almost anything.

- Everyone needs someone with whom to share their secrets.

- Listening is just as important as talking.

- An understanding friend is better than a therapist... and cheaper, too!

- Laughter makes the world a happier place.

- Friends are like wine; they get better with age.

- Calories don't count when you are having lunch (or any other food) with your girlfriends.

- Sometimes you just need a shoulder to cry on.

- Great minds think alike, especially when they are female!

- When it comes to "bonding," females do it better.

- You are never too old for a slumber party!

- Girls just want to have fun.

- It's important to make time to do "girl things."

- You can never have too many shoes.

- Gems may be precious, but friendship is priceless!
  — Author Unknown

My Girlfriends and Me

We've been friends through a million things —
in our worst moments
when everything seemed horrible
and on our best days
when every moment was beautiful.

We've shared all our thoughts,
    our dreams, and our hearts.
We've kept each other's secrets
    and sworn to be faithful.

We've spent time revealing
   the deepest part of our feelings
and encouraging each other
   when one of us was insecure.

We've been each other's strength
   during the saddest moments
and shared each other's dreams through
   every change or discouragement.

We've been the best of friends —
we know each other better
   than anyone else,
and we accept each other.

We've shared a lot through the years,
   and I will always love my girlfriends.

— Regina Hill

With a Girlfriend...

- You can just be yourself.

- You don't have to worry about looking your best — she already knows you're beautiful inside and out.

- You don't have to try to impress her — she already loves you for the person you are.

- You don't have to pretend you're happy when you're upset — she can already tell how you're feeling just by looking at you.

- Girlfriends love to pass themselves off as sisters, regardless of obvious differences in age, size, shape, and skin tone.

- They can have a disagreement one minute and double over in fits of laughter the next.

- They will hold your hand when you need support and give you high-fives when you've done something you're proud of.

- Without your girlfriend, you don't feel complete.

Our Girlfriends Are the Family We Chose for Ourselves

Both within the family and without, our sisters hold up our mirrors, our images of who we are and of who we can dare to become.

— Elizabeth Fishel

Family is a feeling
of belonging and acceptance.
It's a safe retreat, a shelter,
and an instant connection
to the people who have faith in you —
a wonderful circle of lifelong friends
whose smiles go straight
to your heart with love.
It's a special source of well-being —
full of people who hold you
    in the roughest times,
share your life,
and love to be there for you.

— Barbara J. Hall

The Gift of
a Sister's Love

We didn't have all those yesterdays
of being little girls together.
We didn't share the same
mother and father
or help each other blow out
our birthday candles.
There weren't any days of playing
hopscotch or tag,
of staying up nights giggling
and planning our future.
We never shared in the gift of love
that only sisters can, until now.

I have been so lucky in having had
a life filled with many friends,
but none of them knows my heart
and my spirit the way my best girlfriend does.
She has given me something very special,
a gift I never knew I had missed,
and which now
I can't imagine being without...
the gift of a sister's love.

— Joan Benicken

My Girlfriends Are like Angels to Me

In this life, on this earth, and in the days that I spend trying to do the best I can, I know that I wouldn't be half the person I am if it weren't for a little divine inspiration that comes from having girlfriends. They have been my saving grace on more than one occasion.

They are my see-me-through and inspire-my-smile companions. When they listen, they hear what I'm really trying to say. And when they communicate, their words come straight from the heart. They make me feel that "yes, my presence really does matter!" They constantly add to my joys and to the value of my self-worth, and I wish I could thank them every day.

My girlfriends are my very own down-to-earth angels. I cherish them very much, and I am grateful for the joy they bring to my life.

— Marin McKay

A Special Bond

It is so very hard
to find someone in your life
that you can become close to
and friends with.
It takes a special bond
to bring two people together —
a lot of patience
and understanding,
a sprinkle of mischief for
    the good times,
and an abundance of laughter.

— Nanci Brillant

You can tell when two women are close friends. They have a strange way of finishing each other's sentences, beginning to laugh about an old joke long before the punch line, communicating with their eyes, or contentedly sitting in silence with a sense of complete understanding.

— Jane Andrews

Promises Between Girlfriends

I promise that I'll thank every wishing star that ever shined for bringing your closeness and understanding to me.

I promise that nothing will ever change the amount of appreciation I have for you. I promise that if I ever have news to share, you'll always be first on the call list. I promise if I ever release a genie from a magic lamp, I'll share my three wishes with you. In the event that never happens, I promise that you're welcome to split any pizza I might have in my possession. (And the same goes for chocolate.)

I promise I will be there to see you through anything that tries to get you down. I promise that I'll be around through it all, I'll support you in your efforts, and I'll believe in you at all times. We'll do whatever it takes, and together we'll chase away the clouds and keep the sun shining in our lives. When you need to be around someone who truly appreciates your crazy sense of humor, I will gladly, happily, and joyfully be that person.

I'll never take the beauty of our friendship for granted, and I'll never stop trying to tell you how much you mean to me.

I promise.

— L. N. Mallory

Old Friends

There is nothing like an old friend.
With old friends, the only requirement
is that you be yourself.
You can say whatever is on your mind
and do whatever you feel like doing.
You never have to worry,
because you know your friendship
is not based on perfection,
but on respect and acceptance.

With old friends,
you can share the most intimate
and important aspects of yourself,
knowing that their beauty and value
will be recognized and appreciated.

With old friends,
distance has no meaning or power.
There's a bridge made of
love and memories, joys and sorrows,
that connects old friends and keeps them close.

With old friends, you feel safe.
They've been there for you
through the roughest storms,
so you know you can trust them,
believe in them, and count on them.
You know they will be at your side,
so there is peace within your heart.

With old friends, you never feel lonely,
because the roots that bind you
have grown deep and strong.
Your friendship has withstood
the test of time.

— Nancye Sims

Best Friends

A best friend is that one special person
you can lean on and laugh with,
the one you can always turn to no matter
what's going on in her world or yours.

A best friend helps you discover
a little more about yourself every day
because she always encourages you to share
who you are and what you are feeling.

A best friend accepts you at all times.
She doesn't only love you because,
she loves you in spite of.
She cares about your happiness
as much as she cares about her own.
She stands beside you
when others walk away.

A best friend never stops believing in you,
even if you stop believing in yourself.
She has the smile that hugs you,
the laughter that heals your heartaches,
and the words that always lift your spirit.

A best friend is
a one-in-a-million find,
the pot of gold at the end of the rainbow,
a treasure that gives you wealth untold.

— Vickie M. Worsham

Friends for Life

When we are old women
we will sit on the porch
and watch the leaves tremble
in autumn's breath
We will rock on rocking chairs
the lull of aged wood
creaking under our feet
We will wear pretty dresses
with purple flowers in our hair
and hum songs in our heads
to the beat of children's laughter
in the distance

We will say nothing at times
and that silence will be
our greatest solace
and other times we will talk for hours
or until the sun sinks into night
and the moon comes out to play
We will remember then
the days when life was defined
by complexity
when we danced in the moonlight
until the sun came out
and when we vowed our friendship
would last a lifetime

— Deana Marino

Girlfriends Are There for Each Other in Good Times and Bad

To help one another is part of the religion of our sisterhood.

— Louisa May Alcott

My special friends
are the ones who
have walked beside me,
comforting my spirit or
holding my hand
when I needed it the most.
They were friends who
loved my smiles
and were not afraid of my tears.
They were true friends
who really cared about me.
Those friends are forever;
they are cherished and loved
more than they'll ever know.

— Deanna Beisser

When You're Sad...

- ◉ A girlfriend feels your pain.

- ◉ She comforts you with kind words and warm hugs.

- ◉ She brings you a pint of your favorite ice cream and a spoon.

- ◉ She helps you put things in perspective.

- ◉ She does whatever it takes to make you feel better.

When You're Happy...

- A girlfriend shares in your joy.

- She does a "happy dance" with you.

- She reminds you that you deserve all the happiness in the world.

- She takes you out to celebrate.

- She does whatever it takes to make your happiness last.

Girlfriends Share Secrets, Laughter, and Dreams

Girls especially are fond of exchanging confidences with those whom they think they can trust; it is one of the most charming traits of a simple, earnest-hearted girlhood, and they are the happiest women who never lose it entirely.

— Lucy Larcom

If you've got secrets you want to tell, we can talk all day long. If your dreams get broken somehow, I'll remind you that you belong. If you need someplace to hide, you can hold my hand for a while. If your sky begins to fall, I'll stay with you till you smile. Whenever you need some space, there's my room — you can take it. If someone breaks your heart, together we'll unbreak it. When you feel sad or empty inside, I'll show you you're not alone. If you get lost out there, I'll come and take you home. I'll go with you somewhere else, when you need to get away. And when nothing seems to be going right and you need a friend... I'll stay.

— Ashley Rice

When Times Are Tough, Talk to Your Girlfriends

My girlfriend is
the one I tell my troubles to,
the one who listens carefully
and always understands.
There have been so many times when
I gave her all my fears and hurts,
and each time she gave back a heart
filled with love and concern,
a shoulder to rest my worries upon,
and a tranquility found nowhere else
    on earth.

She's the friend who means so much to me,
the one I'm thinking of right now,
the one who feels like family in my heart.

— Barbara J. Hall

Sometimes we do not feel
like we want to feel
Sometimes we do not achieve
what we want to achieve
Sometimes things happen
that do not make sense
Sometimes life leads us in directions
that are beyond our control
It is at these times most of all
that we need someone
who will quietly understand us
and be there to support us
I want you to know
that I am here for you
in every way
and remember that though
things may be difficult now
tomorrow is a new day

— Susan Polis Schutz

Strong Women

Strong women are those who know the road ahead will be strewn with obstacles, but they still choose to walk it because it's the right one for them.

Strong women are those who make mistakes, who admit to them, learn from those failures, and then use that knowledge.

Strong women are easily hurt, but they still extend their hearts and hands, knowing the risk and accepting the pain when it comes.

Strong women are sometimes beat down by life, but they still stand back up and step forward again.

Strong women are afraid. They face fear and move ahead to the future, as uncertain as it can be.

Strong women are not those who succeed the first time. They're the ones who fail time and again, but still keep trying until they succeed.

Strong women face the daily trials of life, sometimes with a tear, but always with their heads held high as the new day dawns.

— Brenda Hager

An Inspiration and a Blessing

My girlfriend is the one
I turn to when I need help,
knowing that —
no matter how much
or what kind —
it will be given
without exception.

She is the one
I think of first
when I hear a good joke
or a great piece of gossip.

She is the one
with whom I really can just be myself,
regardless of who or what
my real self is.

She is the one
who will listen to me
when I know that what I'm saying
is nonsense,
but I want someone to
listen to me anyway,
and who is there when I'm hurting
so much that it seems like
nothing will ever be right again.

She is the one
who can comfort me
when I'm in trouble, scared,
alone, confused, or sad;
who shares with me a bond
that no other two people can share;
who is always there for whatever reason.

She is an inspiration and a blessing in my life.

— Tracey A. Gibbs

Girlfriends Help Us Remember What Is Most Important...

It's not having everything go right;
it's facing whatever goes wrong.
It's not being without fear;
it's having the determination
   to go on in spite of it.

It's not where you stand,
but the direction you're going in.
It's more than never having bad moments;
it's knowing you are always
   bigger than the moment.

It's believing you have already
    been given everything
you need to handle life.
It's not being able to rid
    the world of all its injustices;
it's being able to rise above them.
It's the belief in your heart
    that there will always be
more good than bad in the world.

It's remembering to live just this one day
and not add tomorrow's troubles
    to today's load.
It's remembering that every day ends
and brings a new tomorrow
full of exciting new things.
It's loving what you do,
    doing the best you can,
and always remembering
    how much you are loved.

— Vickie M. Worsham

A Girlfriend Is...

- A confidante.

- A sounding board.

- A shopping buddy.

- A shining star.

- An inspiration.

- A guardian angel.

- A role model.

A girlfriend is a reminder of the blessings that come from closeness. Sharing secrets. Disclosing dreams. Learning about life together.

— Mia Evans

A girlfriend is a steady stream of support, a reassuring feeling that is always with you, and a gift whose value is immeasurable. She is beautiful in more ways than she will ever know.

— K. D. Stevens

Words to Help a Girl Get Through the Day

Stay positive! (Hopeful people are happier people.) Choose wisely. (Good choices will come back to bless you.) Remember what matters. (The present moment. The good people in it. Hearts and dreams and feelings.) Don't stress out over things you can't control. (Just don't.) Count every blessing. (Even the little ones add up to a lot.)

And truly understand these three things:

- How special you are.
- How strong you can be.
- And how, YES, you are going to make it through, no matter what.

You may not be dancing in the streets or jumping on the bed... but you're going to get through the day, the night, and each and every moment that lies ahead. You stay strong, girl!

— Marin McKay

Girlfriends Share...

- ◉ Inside jokes.

- ◉ Meaningful conversations.

- ◉ Tons of laughter.

- ◉ Clothes, shoes, and accessories.

- ◉ Chocolate-chip cookies. (And sometimes just the cookie dough!)

- ◉ So many great memories.

- ◉ A bond that cannot be broken.

- The friendship girlfriends share is sacred, intricate, and unique. It's one of the most important relationships they'll ever have.

- Without girlfriends, the world would be a lonely place.

- Girlfriends sit on park benches and remember the good-old days.

- They can read each other's mind and finish each other's sentences.

- A girlfriend is like home.

A Thank-You to My Girlfriend

Thank you for all the warmth,
for the listening that goes deeper
than hearing my spoken words.
Thank you for gentle advice and for
sharing smile-making remedies that
can cure any case of the blues.
Thank you for truly, absolutely inspiring me,
for giving me enough leeway to be
a little crazy without ever
holding it against me,
and for letting me know that the bridge
that exists between us will rise
above whatever comes along.

— Ann Turrell

Thank you for being a generous soul
and a beautiful spirit in a world
that could use a million
more people just like you.

Thanks so much for everything
you've done and for all
that you continue to do.

You're appreciated
more than words can say.

— J. Kalispell

Girlfriend, You Deserve the Best!

There are some people in life who bring out the best in you. With them, you're able to say whatever's on your mind; you laugh and connect with them in a way that's so easy and unforced.

In my life, you're one of those people. When I think of you, I can't help but feel happier, more full of energy, and ready to have some fun.

I've spent some of the best times of my life with you, and you will forever be a part of my fondest memories.

— E. D. Frances

People like you make the world
    a better place,
because you think of ways
to make a positive difference
    in the lives of others.

People like you make
those you come in contact with
    feel special
by acts of kindness and deeds
    of thoughtfulness.

You deserve the best out of life,
because that's what you give.
May your kindness and good deeds
always come back to you.

— Barbara Cage

You Are a Truly Remarkable Woman

You are a remarkable woman
who accomplishes so much as a
strong woman
in a man's world
You are strong but soft
strong but caring
strong but compassionate

You are a remarkable woman
who accomplishes so much
as a giving woman
in a selfish world
You give to your friends
to your family
to everyone

You are a remarkable woman
and you are loved by so many people
whose lives you have touched
including mine
— Susan Polis Schutz

Time Only Deepens Our Friendship

I remember when we first became friends
and how wonderful
it felt as our friendship
deepened over time.
We both discovered that
we could tell each other anything
and know we would find
compassion and acceptance.
I'm grateful for each time
my girlfriend was there when I needed her,
and I am deeply thankful for
the kindness she's given so freely.
I've called on her in some of
the darkest and brightest times in my life.

I've revealed my fears
      and heartaches to her,
and she's given me the strength
      to bear them.
I've shared my hopes
and hard-won achievements with her,
and in her I found someone who
      believed in me all along.
No matter how much time passes,
I hope she knows that her
friendship is a gift
      beyond measure.

— Susan Shone

Many people will walk in and out of your life, but only true friends will leave footprints in your heart.

— Eleanor Roosevelt
(attributed)

The wonderful memories my girlfriend and I made over the years will forever be cherished in my heart — the laughter that has filled our lives and lifted us up, the goofy way we can poke fun at each other's quirky habits. "Boring" is a word I've never used as long as we've been friends; even during difficult times, she manages to keep the smiles coming.

Her friendship is one of the reasons this world is a better place to wake up to. I always look forward to the time we spend together — shopping, eating out, small talk over a cup of coffee. These little things really mean a lot to friends.

— Tracy Nash

She'll Always Be a Part of Me

No matter where I am
or what I am doing,
when my girlfriend comes to mind
a smile comes to my face
and a warmth settles in my heart.

The day we met
will always be cherished.
We've grown together,
done a lot together,
and no matter what,
we always let each other know
that we do love and care about each other.

She's more than just a friend to me,
and I hope we never let go
of what we share,
because whether it's across the miles
or just a short distance,
she is and will always be
a part of my life and me.

— Betsy Gurganus

Girlfriends Are Special

Special people touch our lives with their thoughtfulness and sensitivity. They're as good as their word. They give their time free of charge. They really practice the Golden Rule. They'll always be close to us because they're so considerate, helpful, and likable.

Special people reach out and reach back, asking nothing in return. Their words and actions prove time and again that there's no way we could ever repay them. They are always going out of their way for us, without our even asking. They're easy to be with and a joy to be around.

They're there when we need them, just as we try to be
there for them when they need us. They share their
hopefulness, appreciation, and friendliness. We find them
in our thoughts and prayers a lot because they give so
much of themselves and care so much — and that is
why they're loved so much.

— Donna Fargo

For All My Girlfriends

May you be blessed
with all these things...

A little more joy,
a little less stress,
a lot more recognition of
your wonderfulness.

Abundance in your life,
blessings in your days,
dreams that come true,
and hopes that stay.

A rainbow on the horizon,
an angel by your side...
and everything
that could ever bring
a smile to your life.

— Mia Evans

Girlfriends Live in Each Other's Heart... Just like Family

Girlfriends walk through life together, whether they live close or far apart. They know that the other one is there... to share the highs and the lows and everything else.

Girlfriends are connected at the heart, and their commitment to their friendship is permanent. They believe in each other. They are sensitive and supportive, and they can talk about things they may not even talk to their families about. Each of them knows the other will understand, no matter what.

Girlfriends aren't afraid to break the rules, defend each other, and go out of their way. They've cried together and laughed together, and they have been there when it mattered. Their loyalty is strong and lasting, and their bond is unquestionable and unconditional. They know that they'll keep on being there through everything life has in store for them.

No one can take the place of girlfriends. They live in each other's heart... just like family.

— Donna Fargo

ACKNOWLEDGMENTS

We gratefully acknowledge the permission granted by the following authors and authors' representatives to reprint poems or excerpts from their publications.

Susan Polis Schutz for "Thank You for Being My Friend," "Rare People," "To a Special Friend," "You Are a Truly Remarkable Woman," and "Sometimes we do not feel..." Copyright © 1982, 1983, 1984, 1986 by Stephen Schutz and Susan Polis Schutz. And for "Knowing that you are always here..." and "You know how I feel...." Copyright © 1972 by Continental Publications, renewed copyright © 2000 by Stephen Schutz and Susan Polis Schutz. And for "There is no need for an outpouring...." Copyright © 1976 by Continental Publications, renewed copyright © 2002 by Stephen Schutz and Susan Polis Schutz. All rights reserved.

PrimaDonna Entertainment Corp. for "Our Girlfriends Keep Us Sane," "Girlfriends Live in Each Other's Heart... Just like Family," "Girlfriends Are Special," and "Girlfriends Speak a Language Only Women Understand" by Donna Fargo. Copyright © 2006, 2010, 2011 by PrimaDonna Entertainment Corp. All rights reserved.

A careful effort has been made to trace the ownership of selections used in this anthology in order to obtain permission to reprint copyrighted material and give proper credit to the copyright owners. If any error or omission has occurred, it is completely inadvertent, and we would like to make corrections in future editions provided that written notification is made to the publisher:

BLUE MOUNTAIN ARTS, INC., P.O. Box 4549, Boulder, Colorado 80306.